THE GIANT ALEXANDER IN AMERICA

WELCOME
UNARD
FREI

THE GIANT ALEXANDER IN AMERICA

Story by
FRANK HERRMANN
Pictures by
GEORGE HIM

Puffin Books

To
the lady librarians of England
and America

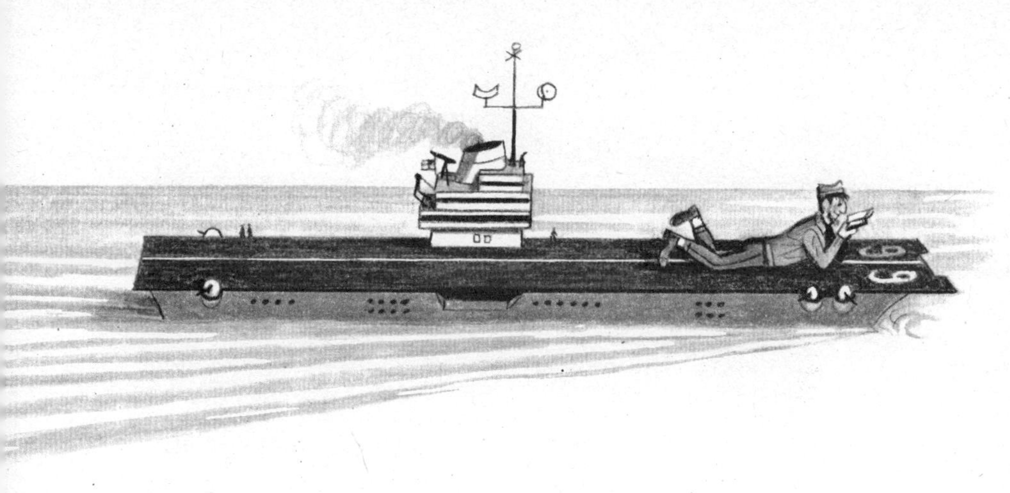

The Giant Alexander was on his way to America by aircraft carrier. The last few days had been very exciting. First his great friend Timmy Dew, who was nine years old and lived next door, had brought him a telegram. It was from the President. It said, "Need your help. Will you come?"

Alexander cabled back, "Of course. Finding ship."

As he was sixty feet tall he couldn't travel on an ordinary ship, so his old friend Coastguard Pennock had rung up the First Lord of the Admiralty in London and told him the problem. "Go to Plymouth with the giant," his Lordship had said, "and meet me at the docks tomorrow at noon."

Alexander had packed a few clothes into a kit bag and said goodbye to Timmy. He promised to send him lots of picture postcards from America.

Now he had been on the aircraft carrier for two days. He had marvellous food because there were four special cooks to cook for him. He loved being at sea. At night he curled up like a cat and a lift took him down to where the planes were usually kept, so that he could sleep safe and sound.

One morning on the voyage he saw some curious lumps in the distance. They seemed to be spouting water. He counted eight, nine, ten, eleven of them. They came closer and closer. Then he realized what they were – whales. He had *always* wanted to meet a whale.

MENU
A

He asked the captain. "Could you stop a moment? I want to talk to those whales."

"It's most unusual," the captain said.

"I promise I won't be long," said Alexander, "but this is a chance in a lifetime."

"All right," said the captain.

Alexander took off his clothes, put on his bathing trunks, and did a beautiful dive into the sea. He reached the whales very quickly. They were rather astonished.

"Good afternoon," said Alexander to the biggest whale, who looked at him in a very friendly way out of his tiny eyes.

“Are you a man?” asked the whale. “Well, sort of,” Alexander replied. “Just rather a big one. What are *you* all doing here?”

“We’re off on a holiday,” said the whale. “It’s been a terrible winter. We need some sunshine and warmth.”

“I am on my way to America,” said Alexander.

“It’s a lovely place,” said the whale. “We went there the year before last. Some of the beaches look fabulous!” The other whales had formed a circle round Alexander and they all had a good chat.

"It has been delightful to meet you," said Alexander. "I had always wanted to see someone as big as myself, and you are."

"And I had always wanted to talk to a man," said the whale. "I didn't know they came as big as you. If you ever need any help let me know."

"How shall I contact you?" asked Alexander.

"Find any dolphin and ask him for Fernandez."

All the whales waved their tails and Alexander swam back to the aircraft carrier.

Two days later they arrived in New York. They went very slowly so that when Alexander stood on the deck he could see all the sights. They docked near Forty-fourth Street. The giant felt tiny when he saw all those huge buildings. But he was very glad to be back on land, because he hadn't been able to take much exercise on the aircraft carrier.

He was welcomed to America by the Mayor of New York. Imagine his surprise when he saw Timmy standing beside the Mayor.

"What are you doing here?" he asked Timmy.

"I am going to help you," Timmy said. "The Admiralty thought you might find things a bit difficult in a strange country, so they gave me a holiday and let me off from school."

"Splendid," said the giant. "Come to your usual place," and he put Timmy in his top pocket.

"Can we look round New York?" he asked the Mayor.

"Just a very quick look," the Mayor replied, "then we'll have to go straight to Washington. The President is most anxious to see you. This way." People were astonished to see the giant but they were delighted when he waved to them. Many of the children knew all about Alexander because they had read about him in the newspapers.

DRUGS

Alexander and Timmy crossed to the other side of the Hudson River and there, waiting for them, was the biggest car-transporter they had ever seen. Alexander sat on it and used his kit bag as a cushion. Six policemen on motorcycles rode in front and six behind.

In what seemed no time at all they reached Washington. They saw the Potomac River sparkling in the sun, the huge Capitol, the Monument to Washington and then they arrived at the White House. The President was waiting to speak to Alexander from the roof.

"I'm very glad you've come, Mr. Alexander," he said. "I want to get our man on the moon as soon as possible. My scientists say you can help them."

"Is it something to do with rockets?" the giant asked. "I hate loud noises."

"Yes, it is connected with rockets," the President replied. "But you will get special ear-mufflers. You'll hardly hear a thing."

"Oh good," the giant sighed with relief.

"Is that your friend Timmy Dew?" the President asked, looking at Timmy's head peeping out of Alexander's top pocket.

"Yes indeed," the giant said. "He is a great help to me."

"Let me shake him by the hand," the President said, "and wish you both a happy time while you are in America."

The car-transporter soon took Alexander and Timmy Dew to Cape Kennedy where all the big rockets are launched. A very nice-looking man with thick horn-rimmed spectacles waved to them outside a big shed just about the size of Alexander's home in Maldon, Essex. "Welcome to Cape Kennedy," he said. "My name is Eugene MacWhirter, and I am going to look after you while you are here. This is where you will live."

It was the most wonderful house Alexander had ever seen. There was a very comfortable living room with a huge, comfortable chair (and little ones for Timmy Dew and ordinary-sized visitors); there was an enormous bed in the bedroom (and a little one for Timmy Dew); and there were even two baths—a vast one for Alexander and a small one for Timmy.

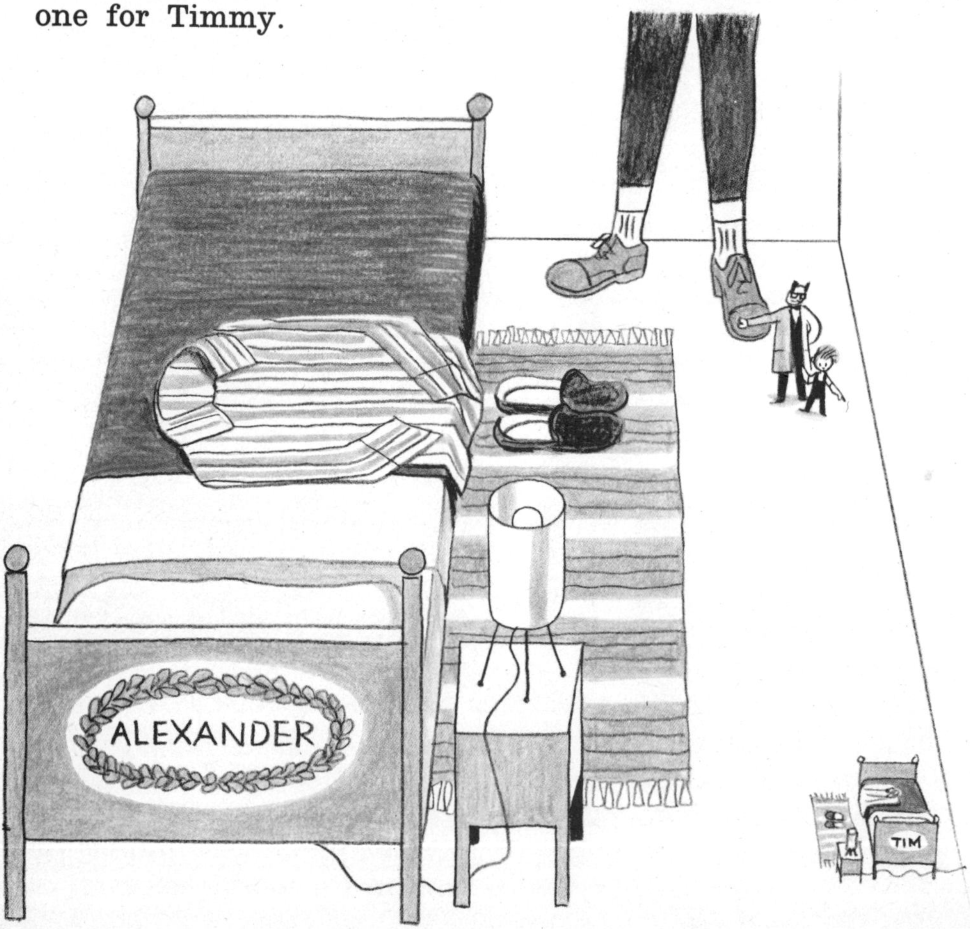

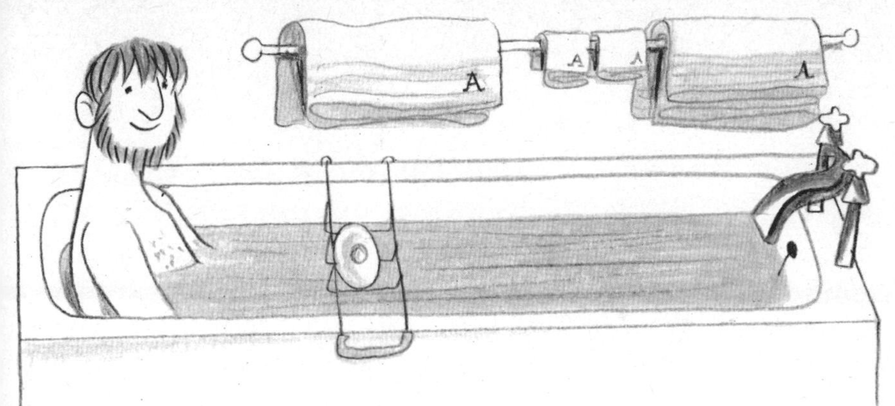

After Timmy and Alexander had had lunch, Mr. MacWhirter looked at them very seriously and said, "I expect you are wondering what we want you to do. Well, it's very simple. You, Alexander, are sixty feet tall, which is about ten times as big as ordinary people. The earth is almost ten times as big as the moon. So when you walk or run or jump, it feels a bit as it will when a man gets on the moon. So we want to study how you move."

Alexander thought it was very surprising that anyone found this interesting. But, after all, he had come all the way to America because the scientists said that they needed him.

Mr. MacWhirter showed Alexander and Timmy round Cape Kennedy. The giant was absolutely amazed. There were buildings so big that he felt quite lost in them, and this had never happened to him before. The biggest building was the one from which a spacecraft would be launched to the moon.

In the end Mr. MacWhirter took the giant to a special shed where people were going to watch him moving. The floors were made of very soft foam rubber, and Alexander had to change into special clothes with lots and lots of wires attached to them. Mr. MacWhirter was pulled up high and spoke to Alexander through a loudspeaker.

"Please do exactly what I tell you. Even if you think it's silly. If you feel too tired to go on, just let me know."

Poor Alexander! He didn't know what he had let himself in for. He had to stand still, sit down, get up, sit down, get up and jump, sit down, get up, jump, run, walk, sit down, roll over and over, sit up, stand up, run some more, and then jump and jump and jump until his lungs were nearly bursting. Timmy Dew felt very sorry for him. And all the time film cameras were photographing everything the giant did, and thirty-seven men in white coats were watching and writing down notes.

"Thank you very much indeed," said Mr. MacWhirter at last. "That was splendid. You can rest now."

The next day the same thing happened; and the next day, and the day after that. The giant was getting quite thin with all the exercise. He said to Mr. MacWhirter, "The President said all this was to do with firing rockets and I was going to have special ear-mufflers. Can I watch a rocket being fired soon?"

"As a matter of fact," said Mr. MacWhirter, "we shall

be launching a rocket in a week's time. Why don't you and Timmy have a holiday till then?"

"That's a jolly good idea," Alexander said. He was very relieved not to have to do any more running and jumping.

They travelled towards the West coast. Timmy had no idea that America was so big. It went on and on and there was always more: Florida, Alabama, Mississippi, Oklahoma, Colorado, Arizona. Here Alexander had the surprise of his life.

Very early one morning Mr. MacWhirter said "You must walk a short way now."

They crossed a strip of hot arid desert. Suddenly Alexander stopped and yelled, "Look, Timmy, look!" And he lifted Timmy up on to his shoulders.

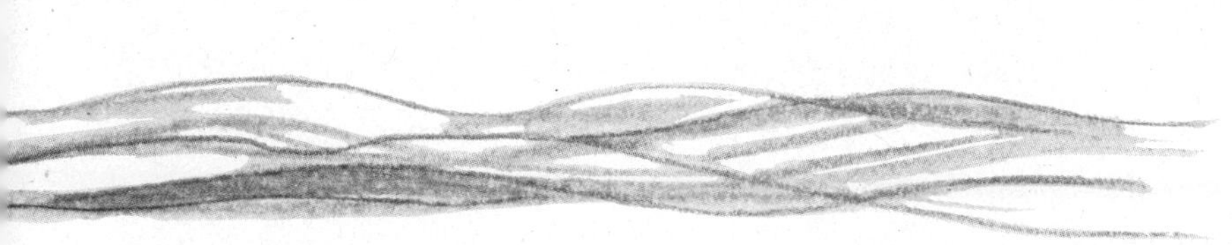

It was the biggest hole in the ground they had ever seen. It went down and down and down. It was long too, and at the bottom there seemed to be a tiny trickle of water. And the rocky sides were of the most beautiful colours, lots and lots of them, glistening in the sunlight.

"It's what's called the Grand Canyon," Mr. MacWhirter explained, "and the river at the bottom is the Colorado."

Alexander wanted to climb right down to the bottom but Mr. MacWhirter wouldn't let him. He was worried that Alexander might twist his ankle. So they sadly got back on to their car-transporter and continued their journey.

After lunch that day the sky became dark; it got quite cold and it started to pour with rain. Timmy had never seen rain like it. There were mountains on both sides of the road and the wind seemed to shriek between them. They heard great rumbles in the distance.

At last the rain stopped, but they hadn't gone many miles when they saw a long line of cars and buses held up in front of them. A huge landslide of earth and rocks had blocked the road. But that wasn't all. A tremendous herd of cattle seemed to be stuck on the other side. The steers were bellowing wildly and men were shouting. Only Alexander was able to look over the top of the landslide. He saw that the herd was trapped between the road and a deep, swirling river. The herd was heading

straight for the river. The cowboys on their horses didn't seem able to stop it. Alexander put Timmy in his top pocket and vaulted over to the other side. Before men or cattle could get over their astonishment at seeing him, he picked up the leading steers, two at a time, and put them down a long way from the river. After he had moved about twenty, the cowboys managed to turn the rest of the herd. The cattle were saved.

The cowboys hardly knew what to say. They were so relieved. The giant smiled at them in his quiet way and said, "I must clear the road now," and began to move the huge rocks. When the motorists on the other side realized what he was doing, they cheered like mad and began to move the smaller lumps of rock as well. In a couple of hours the road was clear.

After two more days of holiday, they returned to Cape Kennedy. They got back just in time for the launching of the rocket. There were two men, called astronauts, in the spacecraft. They were going to walk out into space. It was very exciting, though Timmy and Alexander had to watch from a long way off. It took ages because at first little things kept going wrong. People were endlessly counting. Timmy and Alexander heard it through special earphones under their ear-mufflers. Then, "nine, eight, seven, six, five, four, three, two, one, zero, ignition, BLAST-OFF!" There was a long low rumble, a lot of

smoke, a lot of flame. The tower holding the rocket swayed and wobbled, but it was a good launch. The rocket soared up into the sky—as straight as straight.

After the rocket had disappeared Alexander came into a special assembly shed, took off his protective clothes, and listened to what was happening in the control room.

At first everything went exactly as planned. Then everybody got very worried. Mr. MacWhirter explained that all the big ships that were going to pick up the spacecraft from the sea had been delayed by a storm that had blown up from nowhere. The ships were not going to get to the right place in the sea in time.

"Where is it?" Alexander shouted. "Write it down for me, Timmy." He tore the piece of paper from Timmy's

hand and rushed towards the beach. In a few minutes he had swum a long way out into the sea. Then he spotted a whole lot of dolphins. "Find Fernandez the whale, as quickly as you can," he bellowed at them, "and tell him and his friends that Alexander wants him to pick up a round metal barrel that will fall into the sea from the sky at four o'clock this afternoon." And he told the dolphins exactly where Fernandez should go.

Then he went for a long, refreshing swim to catch up with the U.S. naval ships. Meanwhile Timmy had guessed what Alexander was going to do, because the giant had told him of his meeting with the whales. Timmy explained to Mr. MacWhirter that he and the other scientists need not worry any more.

Sure enough Fernandez got the message, and at five minutes to four he and the other ten whales were in exactly the right place. When the space capsule fell into the sea, Fernandez and the second-biggest whale swam close together and carried it along on their backs. The astronauts inside were flabbergasted when they saw what was happening, but they were very happy that they had been rescued.

After an hour the whales reached the ships. Alexander was on an aircraft carrier. He picked the capsule off the whales' backs and lowered it gently on to the deck. Then he let out the two astronauts. The sailors on the ship cheered Alexander and the whales.

"Thank you so much, Fernandez," Alexander said. "That was terribly nice of you. I didn't know I would need you so soon."

"Not a bit," said Fernandez. "It was a real pleasure. It's given us something to remember our holiday by. See you again soon," and waving their tails again the whales swam off.

All the world had been listening to the radio and hearing about the astronauts' adventure and the way they were rescued. And suddenly everybody knew who the Giant Alexander was and Timmy Dew too, for that matter. So when the pair of them were getting back to New York a few days later, everyone was wild to see them, and Fernandez too! Timmy had a brilliant idea. Why not enter New York from the sea, riding on the whale?

Fernandez was found again and the three of them approached New York in this way.

There had never been such a welcome the whole of New York stopped work while Alexander walked round the city.

At one stage he stopped for five minutes to have a television interview with a reporter on the eighth floor of a skyscraper on Fifth Avenue. "I think America is wonderful," Alexander said. "Timmy does too. But we found it rather hot in Florida. I've got to go home to England tomorrow, but I hope to be back soon."

The giant and Timmy were travelling back on an American aircraft carrier. There was a great surprise just before they left. The President came to say goodbye. He brought them parting presents, which he knew Alexander and Timmy would want for their next visit to America to protect them from the strong sun: a ten-gallon hat for Timmy Dew and a hundred-gallon one for Alexander. It was the biggest hat in the world!